I0791279

This Book Belongs to

Dedicated to

My Husband and Four precious gems Aakash, Adithya, Abishek and Sparsha. You make me so proud. Always be the best you can be.
-Mommy

Credits

Pictures from Google.com labeled for reuse, Bing.com All creative commons, Pixabay. Info from Wildlife fact files

RUBY- THROAT HUMMINGBIRD

RUBY- THROAT HUMMINGBIRD

This beautiful bird is called Ruby Throat Hummingbird.

It gets this name from the male's magnificent blood red throat plumage
RUBY- THROAT HUMMINGBIRD

Order- Apodiformes
Family- Trochilidae
Genus - Archilochus
Species- Colubris
RUBY- THROAT HUMMINGBIRD

RUBY- THROAT HUMMINGBIRD

Its
length is
4 inches

RUBY- THROAT HUMMINGBIRD

Its wingspan is 5 inches

It weighs
about 1/10 oz
RUBY- THROAT HUMMINGBIRD

RUBY- THROAT HUMMINGBIRD
Breeding season is from March-July

RUBY- THROAT HUMMINGBIRD
Has 2 eggs per clutch and is incubated for 16 days
12

It's habitat is woods,
orchards and gardens

It feeds on nectar and insects
RUBY- THROAT HUMMINGBIRD

RUBY- THROAT HUMMINGBIRD 
It's lifespan is 5 years

There are 320 different species in North and South America

RUBY- THROAT HUMMINGBIRD

RUBY- THROAT HUMMINGBIRD

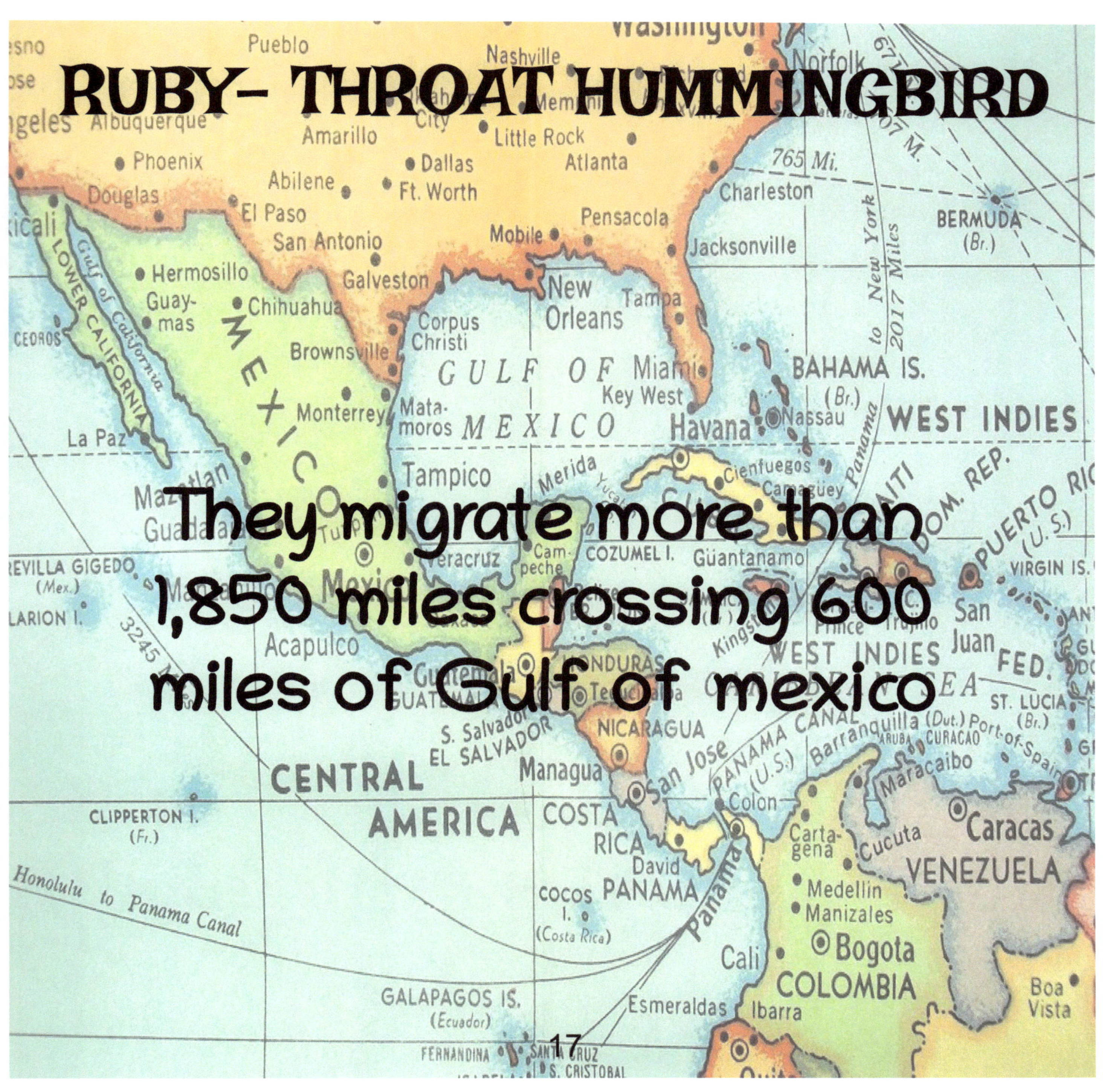

To spend their winter time in Central America
RUBY- THROAT HUMMINGBIRD

<u>Interesting facts</u>

This bird has the smallest number of feathers ever counted on a bird

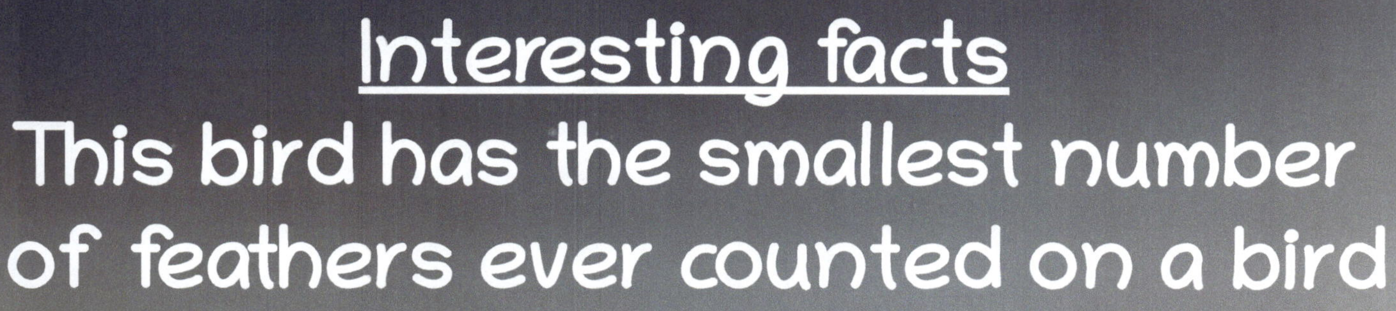

Interesting facts These birds can be caught by dragonflies

RUBY- THROAT HUMMINGBIRD

<u>Interesting facts</u>

These birds can be caught by Spiders

<u>Interesting facts</u> These birds
can snatched by frogs
22

Interesting facts
Before migration these birds produce layers of fat equal to half its body weight
23

Interesting facts
Victorians decorate their living room with the stuffed hummingbirds
24

Interesting facts
Hummingbirds eat food twice its body weight every day
25

Interesting facts
Hummingbirds fly backwards
26

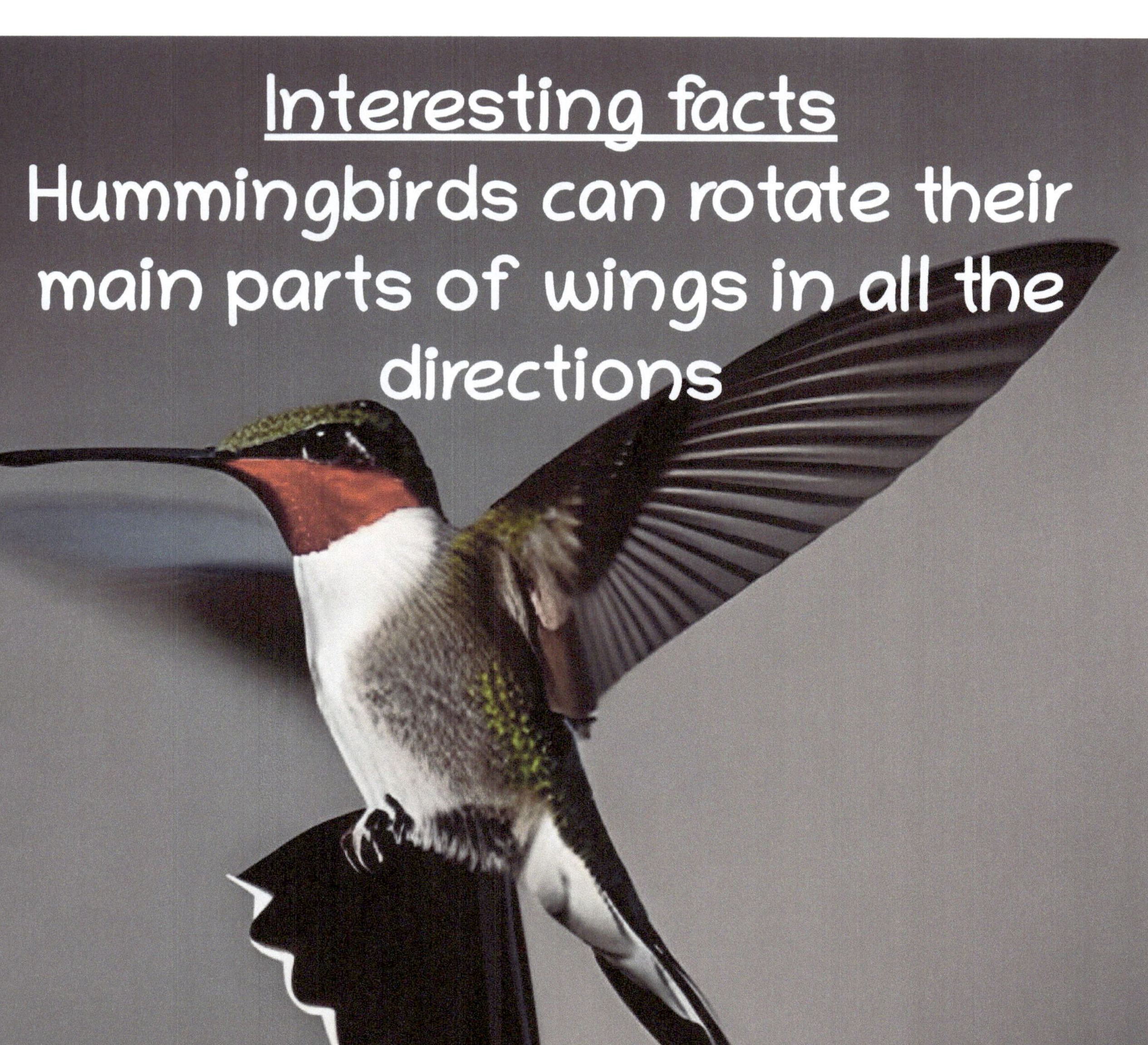

Interesting facts
Hummingbirds can rotate their main parts of wings in all the directions
27

RUBY- THROAT HUMMINGBIRD

Notes

RUBY- THROAT HUMMINGBIRD

Notes

RUBY- THROAT HUMMINGBIRD

Notes

RUBY- THROAT HUMMINGBIRD

Notes

RUBY- THROAT HUMMINGBIRD

Thank you for reading about this beautiful bird -Ruby Throat Hummingbird. Hope you enjoyed it. Check out our next book All about Stingray

www.ingramcontent.com/pod-product-compliance
Lightning Source LLC
Chambersburg PA
CBHW040055240726
48664CB00004B/1197